Wreaths

Wreaths

Carol Endler Sterbenz
Photography by Jennifer Lévy

DORSET PRESS
NEW YORK

A FRIEDMAN GROUP BOOK

Published by Dorset Press
A division of Marboro Books Corporation

ISBN 0-88029-677-1

WREATHS
was prepared and produced by
Michael Friedman Publishing Group, Inc.
15 West 26th Street
New York, New York 10010

Editor: Elizabeth Viscott Sullivan
Designer: Lynne Yeamans
Photography Editor: Christopher C. Bain

Typeset by Bookworks Plus
Color separation by Excel Graphic Arts Ltd.
Printed and bound in Hong Kong by Leefung-Asco Printers Ltd.

For Emily, Louise, and Emilio

Contents

Introduction
* 8 *

Materials and Supplies
* 10 *

Techniques
* 14 *

Design Plans and Strategies
* 18 *

Winter

White and Lavender Wreath
* 21 *

Golden Branch Wreath
* 24 *

Empire Plume Wreath
* 27 *

Vine Wreath with Folk Dolls
* 30 *

Spring

Painted Vine Wreath with Rose Swag
* 33 *

Faux Rose Topiary
* 36 *

Cream and Persimmon Wreath with Print
* 38 *

Miniature Heart and Rings
* 41 *

Cherub with Sweet Pea Wreath
* 44 *

Summer

Garden Rows
* 47 *

Willow Wreath with Berry Swag
* 51 *

Amaranth Bouquet
* 52 *

Heart Wreath with Rose Clusters
* 55 *

Autumn

Angel's Lace Fan with Silk Roses
* 59 *

Vine Wreath with Autumn Strawflowers
* 62 *

Vine Wreath with Grape Clusters
* 64 *

French Horn with Evergreens
* 66 *

Traditional Evergreen Wreath
* 69 *

Further Reading
* 70 *

Sources
* 71 *

Metric Conversion Chart
* 72 *

Index
* 72 *

Introduction

Wreaths is an introduction to wreath making, a completely manageable art form that will allow you to enjoy spring gardens in winter, and to imagine the fragrance of an entire evergreen forest with one hint of scent from a Christmas wreath. No matter what your level of craft experience, you will be able to create any one of the wreath designs in this collection and, in the process, develop the skills and experience necessary to create more complex arrangements. Perhaps you'll even venture beyond the written directions from the wreaths offered here to create designs of your own!

Although most people usually associate wreaths with the winter holiday season, *Wreaths* shows you how to reinterpret the wreath for yearlong display, thanks to a variety of treatments and decoration. A plain vine wreath, for example, can take on a whole new look; painted teal blue, and decorated with clusters of cerise-tinged tea roses, golden yarrow, and cream baby's breath, the wreath may echo a romantic Victorian past, and conjure up images of lace, cut crystal, and silver powder boxes. The same wreath, left unpainted, but adorned with red and black silk berries and ribbon, is certainly a less complex interpretation, but is equally effective in its suggestion of summer's simplicity and bounty.

Inspiration for wreath decoration is all around us—from the settings we place them in to the functions we wish them to serve. An aromatic dried herb wreath can please our eye in the kitchen and provide flavorsome additions to the evening meal. The small wreath ornament used to enhance a gift package can later crown a table napkin. With little previous experience and a few common materials, we can make wreaths to enhance our home, inside and out, and plan our gift giving with wreaths in mind.

The purpose of *Wreaths* is to get you started. The entire collection is based on a few assumptions: that we love beautifully handcrafted objects and we enjoy making them ourselves; and, that although we may wish to start a project from scratch, we know that we are more likely to finish it if we begin somewhere in the middle, given the limits and demands on our time. Hence, most of the wreaths in the collection call for the use of finished wreath forms and ready-made decorative materials easily found at local craft stores and florists. The step-by-step directions are concise but styled to allow creative headroom.

The source directory provides a guide to shops, designers, and mail-order companies that supply the best in ready-made wreaths and floral arrangements, as well as everything you will need to create a wreath of your own. Also included are suggestions for further reading, books that offer more detailed information on the preparation of basic wreath forms as well as a multitude of ways to prepare and use decorative materials.

In all cases, *Wreaths* is an introduction to a creative, fun, and fulfilling craft. You may even find yourself looking at the world in a new way—seeing gems in a late summer garden, rescuing bits of interesting ribbon, or hanging a spring bouquet of dried flowers outside when the back stairs are still wrapped in snow.

Materials and Supplies

In principle, there are two basic components of any wreath: its frame and decoration.

Frames

Frames are classified by the material from which they are constructed. There are four types of wreath frames:

Vine: a natural, gangly, flexible branch that is wound into wreaths with diameters between 6″ and 18″. Vine wreaths are available in natural (with bark or peeled) and in painted finishes, and are strong enough to hold heavy ornamentation.

Wire: a plain or painted metal that is available in many thicknesses (gauges). Wire allows for enormous flexibility. You can make free-form shapes from chicken wire, or hoops of any size from lengths of wire. You can also buy welded frames in diameters between 6″ and 18″. Wire can hold heavy ornamentation.

Foam: a lightweight material available either in blocks that can be carved or glued together (also referred to as oasis), or in flat or curved rings with diameters between 8″ and 24″. Foam provides a flat surface for building up lightweight materials.

Straw: a lightweight, natural, dried-grass material that is packed into ring shapes and bound securely with nylon string. Straw wreaths are available in diameters between 6″ and 18″. Straw provides a solid wreath-making frame, capable of holding moderate-weight ornamentation, and is very well suited for ornamentation on floral picks.

Decoration

Decoration usually consists of a cover material to conceal the wreath frame, such as moss, leaves, ribbon, and paper, as well as the ornamentation, the additional material that decorates the cover

material. The possibilities for decoration are endless, and include just about anything that appeals to you. The wreath frame determines the type of decoration that can be used; heavy decoration requires a strong frame, such as vine or wire, while light decoration can be placed upon a lightweight frame, such as Styrofoam.

Supplies

The supplies used to make the wreaths in this collection are:

* Fine-gauge wire. Used for binding flowers, fine-gauge wire is available on reels
* Medium-gauge wire. Medium-gauge wire is used to form swags and wreath frames
* Craft wire. Craft wire is used to form hanging hooks, and can be affixed to flower stems to make them stiffer
* Floral picks. Floral picks are used to strengthen or lengthen the natural stems of dried flowers
* Floral tape. Floral tape is used to wrap bare stems and wire

Tools

The tools used to make the wreaths in this collection are:

* Florist's scissors
* Wire cutters
* Pruning shears
* Hot-glue gun and glue sticks

Tips on Using a Hot-Glue Gun

Using a hot-glue gun is a highly effective way to achieve a fast, firm bond between materials; however, it should be used with the following cautions:

* Do not leave the gun plugged in when not using it
* Keep a bowl of ice water nearby should you accidentally burn yourself
* Keep children away from the gun

Techniques

Although the majority of wreaths in this collection are designed using finished wreath frames, such as the Heart Wreath with Rose Clusters (p. 55), here are the basic techniques for making your own frames in vine and wire. Also included is a technique for covering wreath frames with moss as well as tips on drying flowers and caring for dried flower arrangements.

Creating a Vine Wreath

To create a vine wreath, collect equal lengths of natural vine. Bend one length of vine into a hoop, overlapping and intertwining the ends. (Remember that the size of your wreath will be determined by the length of this vine.) Temporarily secure the overlapping ends of the vine with wire. Next, intertwine two or three more vines around this main vine in the same way. Continue to add new lengths of vine and weave the loose ends into the main vine until the wreath is the desired thickness. Remove the wire.

Creating a Wire-Frame Garland and Wreath

To create a wire-frame wreath, begin by making a garland, then simply convert the garland to a hoop. To make a garland, arrange your chosen material (flowers, foliage, etc.), with stems cut to size, as well as any other materials that need stems mounted on wire; wire the material into individual corsages and set them aside. Next, cut a length of medium-gauge wire to the desired size; it is helpful to imagine the wire bent into a circle to picture wreath size, and thus appropriate wire length. Wrap the medium-gauge wire with floral tape, making a loop at one end and twisting the loop to secure it. Insert a corsage of flowers or foliage into the loop and bind it in place using fine-gauge wire on a reel. Continue binding corsages to the garland wire, concealing preceding stems with the next corsage. Work to the end of the garland wire, then bend the garland into a hoop, threading the straight wire end into the loop at the other end and twisting it to secure into a wreath.

Covering Wreath Frames with Moss

To cover any frame with moss, such as Spanish or sphagnum moss, arrange sections or sheets of cover material over the wreath form, tucking the overlap in back of the frame and securing it in place with hot glue. Use floral pins or bind matching sewing thread around the frame to secure the moss, adding patches or wads as needed to conceal the frame completely.

Using and Caring for Dried Flowers

Because a large number of wreaths in this collection use dried flowers, here is some general information on air-drying your own flowers, as well as ways to clean and care for your dried floral arrangements.

To air-dry flowers, gather small bunches of cut or freshly picked flowers, and tie their stems together at the ends. Hang the bunches upside down in a dry, dimly lit place until they are dry. Drying time depends on the density of the stems; foliage and flowers usually dry in a day or two, or may take as long as a week.

Silica gel is useful for drying flower heads. First, put a 2- to 3-inch layer of gel on the bottom of an airtight container. Arrange cut flowers with 1-inch stems on the top of the gel, leaving plenty of room between flowers. Gently sprinkle gel around and through the petals, being sure to cover the flowers completely. Flower heads should be placed on the gel as follows: flat flowers such as daisies should be placed upside down; cup-shaped flowers such as roses should be placed right-side up; spiral-shaped flowers such as snapdragons should be placed on their sides. Do not mix different types of flowers, since drying times vary. Carefully remove the dried flower heads with a slotted spoon. For more specific information on using silica gel, refer to books on the subject.

To clean and care for dried floral arrangements, gently dust the flowers and foliage with a soft artist's brush; or, simply blow lightly on the arrangement. Wreaths made of preserved materials do not last forever, but you can prolong their lives and lessen the harsh effects of bright sunlight and humidity by displaying them in a dimly lit area. You may also wish to store certain fragile wreaths in airtight containers (into which ½ cup of silica gel has been added to absorb moisture) and to display them in the less humid months.

To perk up a faded floral arrangement, add new dried flowers in more vivid colors. You can do this by applying a dab of hot glue to the backs of flower heads, then pressing them gently into place on the wreath. Another way to add life to a faded arrangement is to push new dried flower stems into it.

Design Plans and Strategies

When planning your own wreath design, it is important to coordinate the shape, proportion, texture, and color of the wreath frame and all decorative elements. A helpful way to evaluate your design is to choose your wreath form and lay out all your decorative materials on a flat surface. Then arrange and rearrange the elements until you achieve a look you like. If you can, tack or drape the decorations on the wreath frame and hang the wreath on a blank wall to get an overall picture of your design before you do anything permanent. Once you have determined a general direction, begin to decorate your wreath—experiment freely as you go along and allow the decoration to inspire new design directions.

Home decorating magazines are a good source of ideas. Attractive room settings, with their abundance of fabrics and furniture, are easily translated into a palette for wreath form, decorative elements, and style. Study floral arrangements for ideas on contrast in color and texture: A vase of soft pink roses and airy Queen Anne's lace could be the inspiration for your next wreath. Before you go out shopping for material, look around you and notice how nature juxtaposes color and shape: Certain seasons present fabulous natural materials in abundance, such as seed pods, grasses, flowers faded on their stems, twigs, and lush evergreen branches. Collect what you find and store it away. Everything has potential: You can add ribbons, jewelry findings, trims, beads, and other carefully collected treasures as you go along.

You might consider making a miniature version of a favorite design, or of a design that you are still working with. These small wreaths become delightful projects unto themselves and can be used to decorate a gift, crown a table napkin, leave on a bedside table in the guestroom, or encircle the base of a candlestick.

You can display your wreaths all year long—just change the decorations to suit the season and your decorating style. Replace sprays of bittersweet in your vine wreath with traditional evergreen sprays tied with ribbon, or attach a cluster of ivory-colored roses, gilt mistletoe tied in black satin cord, and gold balls for a touch of elegance instead. And while you're thinking about year-round use, why not find new places for your wreaths besides the traditional door, wall, or mantel? Think about placing a wreath on the table for a centerpiece or wrapping a garland around a banister you'd like to accent.

Of course, these ideas are only suggestions, and are intended to help you approach making and displaying wreaths in new and imaginative ways.

Winter

White and Lavender Wreath

Materials:

* Dried flowers: 3 bunches sea lavender; 1 bunch each purple Australian honeysuckle and purple statice; 36 dried rose leaves
* 1 yard French variegated lavender and avocado ribbon
* 2 yards each satin ribbon in two shades of purple

Supplies:

* Floral tape
* Silver glitter
* Wire: medium-gauge; fine-gauge on a reel; craft
* Florist's scissors
* Wire cutters

Note: This project is first formed as a garland, then converted to a wreath.

Directions:

Bind small corsages of sea lavender, using fine-gauge wire. Set aside. To make garland, cut a 32″ length of medium-gauge wire and wrap with floral tape; make a loop at one end by bending wire over and twisting securely. Insert stems of first corsage into loop, binding in place with fine-gauge wire on reel. Continue binding corsages to medium-gauge wire, overlapping stems with next corsage, working entire length of wire to form a garland. To convert garland to wreath, bend garland into a hoop, thread end wire into loop, bend straight end over and twist securely. Fill in any bare spots with individually wired corsages.

To decorate wreath, position and hot-glue plumes of purple Australian honeysuckle and statice in clusters evenly placed throughout wreath foliage. Position and hot-glue rose leaves around floral clusters. To finish, dust wreath with glitter, and wire ribbon bows and streamers to top of wreath. Form a loop for hanging from craft wire and attach to back of wreath.

Golden Branch Wreath

Materials:

- Very slender tree or bush branches
- Natural leaves or foliage
- 1½ yards wide gold metallic ribbon

Supplies:

- Wire: fine-gauge on reel; medium-gauge; craft
- Floral tape
- Gold spray paint
- Florist's scissors
- Wire cutters
- Hot-glue gun and glue sticks

Note: This project is first formed as a swag, then converted to a wreath.

Directions:

To form swag, cut a 54″ length of medium-gauge wire, and wrap it with floral tape to form nonskid surface. Beginning at one end, and working its full length, tightly bind bunches of very slender branches to medium-gauge wire, using fine-gauge wire on a reel. Allow branches to overlap to create thickness and conceal formerly bound branch stems. To convert swag to wreath, bend swag into hoop, overlapping stems and binding securely in place with fine-gauge wire.

Spray wreath with gold paint, making sure to cover all areas; let dry. To prepare decorative leaves or foliage, spray with gold paint; let dry. Using fine-gauge wire, wire gilt leaves or foliage in clusters, then set aside. Tie and hot-glue a 4-loop bow to wreath front, allowing the V-cut streamers to cascade in folds on either side. Hot-glue gilt leaf clusters as desired. Form a loop for hanging from craft wire and attach to back of wreath.

Empire Plume Wreath

Materials:

* 4 packages glittered angel's lace
* 24 gold leaves
* 1 brass jingle bell
* Angel musician or similar ornament
* 1 package filament-threaded gold beads
* 11" beaded chain in gold
* 2 jewelry trims
* 1 yard gold gauze ribbon
* White acrylic paint and small paint brush

Supplies:

* Floral tape
* Wire: fine-gauge on a reel; medium-gauge; craft
* Florist's scissors
* Wire cutters
* Hot-glue gun and glue sticks

Note: Plumes are bound in opposite directions and extended upward to form a swag.

Directions:

Cut a 25″ length of medium-gauge wire and wrap with floral tape; mark midpoint with magic marker. To form first plume, begin 5″ from one end of medium-gauge wire, and bind several stems of angel's lace at a time, using fine-gauge wire and making sure foliage is full and continuous. Work until stems overlap marked midpoint. To form second plume, begin 5″ from unworked half of medium-gauge wire; bind angel's lace to main wire using fine-gauge wire, continuing until stems overlap swag at midpoint. Tightly bind all stems in place at center of swag. Dab white paint on any chipped areas.

To decorate swag, make two sprays of gold leaves, twisting wire stems of each spray together to secure; conceal stems with jewelry trim, hot-glued in place. Position and hot-glue each spray to a plume where stems meet foliage. To form beaded arch, connect free lengths of swag wire at ends, and twist together to secure; hot-glue a strand of gold beads to entire length of wire. To decorate bell, hot-glue lengths of filament-threaded gold beads to bell top in a cascade; wire bell to beaded arch at arch center and hot-glue an 8-loop bow of gold gauze ribbon to bell top. To finish, hot-glue a single gold leaf to bottom of angel's foot, then hot-glue angel to bottom center of swag.

Vine Wreath with Folk Dolls

Materials:

- 12″ vine wreath
- 2 to 3 stems dried hawthorn berries or similar berry
- Folk dolls

Supplies:

- Wire: fine-gauge; craft
- Wire cutters
- Pruning shears
- Miniature clear electric lights

Directions:

Position and wire stems of hawthorn berries in a swag at bottom of wreath. Position and hot-glue folk dolls to wreath as shown. Form loop for hanging from craft wire and attach to back of wreath. Add lights; conceal wires by tucking between vines.

Spring

Painted Vine Wreath with Rose Swag

Materials:

- 8″ painted vine wreath in light teal
- Dried flowers: 15 hybrid tea roses (3 wine-tinged vanilla, 6 vanilla, 6 deep scarlet); sprigs of golden yarrow and green angel's lace; 6 rose petals; 24 rose leaves
- ¾ yard maroon grosgrain ribbon

Supplies:

- Craft wire
- Florist's scissors
- Wire cutters
- Hot-glue gun and glue sticks

Directions:

Arrange and hot-glue roses to top of wreath, placing larger ones in center of arrangement, smaller ones at outside. Fill in spaces around roses with golden yarrow, adding accents of angel's lace, and hot-glue materials on wreath at attractive angles in a spray pattern. Position and hot-glue rosebuds on either side of central design in a narrow line to create a swaglike look. Hot-glue a collar of rose leaves around entire arrangement, and fill in any bare spots with small clusters of golden yarrow and single rose petals. Tie a bow and hot-glue it to wreath, allowing streamers to dangle freely. Using craft wire, form a loop for hanging and attach to back of wreath.

Faux Rose Topiary

Materials:

- Dried flowers: 48 rose buds; 36 rose blooms; sprigs of blue angel's lace; 60 dried rose leaves; 12″-long stem from dried flower
- 1 yard copper gauze ribbon

Supplies:

- Lightweight cardboard
- Craft wire
- Scissors and compass
- Wire cutters
- Hot-glue gun and glue sticks

Directions:

Using a compass and scissors, mark and cut a semicircle with a 6″-radius from cardboard. Hot-glue a collar of overlapping rose leaves around perimeter of semicircle. Hot-glue a veneer of rose blooms and buds; fill in with angel's lace. Hot-glue 12″-long stem to back of treetop, decorating with a bow of long copper streamers. Form a loop for hanging from craft wire and hot-glue to back of treetop.

Cream and Persimmon Wreath with Print

Materials:

- 8″ Styrofoam ring
- 1 package Spanish moss
- Dried flowers: 1 package each sea lavender, persimmon angel's lace, white angel's lace, and cream statice
- Moss-green sewing thread
- 2 yards narrow cranberry satin ribbon
- Full-color print

Supplies:

- Craft wire
- Florist's scissors
- Wire cutters
- Hot-glue gun and glue sticks

Directions:

To cover Styrofoam ring, wad and overlap Spanish moss on ring, and bind in place with sewing thread. To form flower rows, begin at outer border of wreath, cutting, positioning, and hot-gluing white angel's lace to curve, working completely around wreath. Form a second inside row using sea lavender, then a third inside row using persimmon angel's lace. Finish with a final row of statice, working in same manner as first outside row. Fill in any bare spots.

Measure and cut print to size of inside opening of wreath; hot-glue in place. Tie a bow and hot-glue to bottom center of wreath. Form a loop for hanging from craft wire and attach to back of wreath.

Miniature Heart and Rings

Materials:

* Dried flowers: 6 hybrid tea roses (4 wine-tinged vanilla, 2 vanilla); sprigs of golden yarrow, sea lavender, cream statice, purple Australian honeysuckle, and green angel's lace
* 1 package Spanish moss
* Moss-green sewing thread
* 1 yard narrow purple satin ribbon

Supplies:

* Floral tape
* Wire: medium-gauge; craft
* Florist's scissors
* Wire cutters
* Hot-glue gun and glue sticks

Directions:

To make miniature heart frame, cut a 14″ length of medium-gauge wire and bend into a heart shape, twisting ends together to secure. Wrap wire heart with floral tape. To make miniature ring frames, cut two 14″ lengths of medium-gauge wire, and bend each length into a hoop, twisting ends together to secure. Wrap each ring with floral tape. To cover each frame, wad and overlap Spanish moss on each; bind in place with sewing thread and work until frame is completely covered.

To decorate wreaths, arrange and hot-glue dried flowers on each; begin arrangement in center, continue outward, and fill in bare spots with tiny buds or sprigs of foliage. Hot-glue a bow or streamers to each wreath, and using craft wire, attach a wire loop for hanging to the back of each one as well.

Cherub with Sweet Pea Wreath

Materials:

- 3 stems silk sweet peas
- Ceramic angel or similar figurine
- 1½ yards green satin ribbon

Supplies:

- Wire cutters

Directions:

Form a hoop with one stem of sweet peas; weave ends to secure. Intertwine a second and third stem with first stem, arranging flowers, leaves, and tendrils as you go. Tie a bow at bottom of wreath, allowing streamers to hang freely. Place angel so its hands extend over shelf- or mantel-edge; rest wreath on angel's hands.

Summer

Garden Rows

Materials:

- 12″ Styrofoam ring
- 1 package Spanish moss
- Dried flowers: 1 package cranberry caspia; 1/2 package cream statice; 12 deep red hybrid tea roses; 1/4 package blue angel's lace; 2 unopened rose buds; 40 dried rose leaves
- Moss-green sewing thread
- 1 1/2 yards gold gauze ribbon

Supplies:

- Lightweight cardboard
- Craft wire
- Florist's scissors
- Wire cutters
- Hot-glue gun and glue sticks

Directions:

To cover Styrofoam ring, wad and overlap Spanish moss on ring, binding in place with sewing thread. To form backdrop for floral centerpiece, mark and cut a semicircle of cardboard 1″ larger than measurement of wreath opening; hot-glue to back of bottom half of wreath opening.

For garden, beginning with back row, position and hot-glue stems of caspia to cardboard in an even row across its diameter. Continue in same way with second row using stems of cream statice; do a third row of red roses and finish with angel's lace. Make sure flowers graduate in height, and fill in any bare spots.

For leaf swag at bottom of wreath, arrange and hot-glue rose leaves to form a C as shown; glue unopened rose buds in the center of wings. Attach a bow to bottom center of wreath with streamers extending upward in a V. Form a loop for hanging from craft wire and attach to back of wreath.

Willow Wreath with Berry Swag

Materials:

* 10″ peeled willow wreath in twisted rope pattern
* 2 stems silk berries, 1 red, 1 black
* 1 yard hunter green ribbon

Supplies:

* Craft wire
* Wire cutters
* Hot-glue gun and glue sticks

Directions:

To form berry swag, intertwine stems of red and black berries, bending to form a C. Position swag on bottom front of wreath; tuck stems and thread leaves through willow vines, and secure in place with hot glue. Tie ribbon into a bow, and attach to swag center. Form a loop for hanging from craft wire and secure to back of wreath.

Amaranth Bouquet

Materials:

- 8″ Styrofoam ring
- 3 packages dried globe amaranth
- 1½ yards pink silk moirée ribbon

Supplies:

- Floral tape
- Craft wire
- Hot-glue gun and glue sticks

Directions:

To form frame for bouquet, cut Styrofoam ring into two equal semicircles; match up sections and hot-glue the backs together. Wrap frame with floral tape and place on flat surface with round arch facing up. To form bouquet, begin with back row, and position and hot-glue stems of amaranth in tight, even rows across full expanse of arch. Continue with each successive row in same manner, making sure flower heads are visible (save any broken flower heads and stems for use as filler later on).

When all flowers are glued on, go back over bouquet and hot-glue bare stems with loose dried flowers, and fill bare spaces with extra leaves. Tie a bow around stems of bouquet, anchoring each streamer of ribbon in back with a dab of hot glue. Form a loop for hanging with craft wire and attach to back of wreath.

Heart Wreath with Rose Clusters

Materials:

- 12″ moss-covered heart wreath
- Dried flowers: 12 cerise-tinged hybrid tea roses; 1 package golden yarrow; sprigs of purple Australian honeysuckle, green angel's lace, cream and purple statice, and sea lavender; 18 rose leaves
- 2 yards gold gauze ribbon

Supplies:

- Craft wire
- Florist's scissors
- Wire cutters
- Hot-glue gun and glue sticks

Directions:

Position and hot-glue a spray of roses to center of V-shaped contour as shown. Surround roses with golden yarrow, and hot-glue into place. Hot-glue sprigs of honeysuckle, statice, and sea lavender at attractive angles in a spray pattern, making sure to alternate dark and light flowers to create color contrast. Accentuate top of design with rose leaves and sprigs of angel's lace. Tie a 6-loop bow and hot-glue to top, allowing enough length so streamers dangle in curls alongside wreath. Form a loop for hanging with craft wire and attach to back of wreath.

Autumn

Angel's Lace Fan with Silk Roses

Materials:

- 2 packages empire green angel's lace
- 2 stems red silk tea roses
- 3/4 yard red satin ribbon

Supplies:

- Wire: fine-gauge; craft
- Florist's scissors
- Wire cutters

Directions:

Lay bunches of angel's lace on a flat surface, straightening stems and untangling foliage; divide into 5 equal bunches. Using fine-gauge wire, bind each bunch at point where foliage meets stems. Arrange bunches in a fan shape; lash adjacent bunches together where stems meet foliage, then bind all stems together to form main trunk. Bind stems of silk roses to trunk, arranging flowers and leaves in a spray. With wire cutters, trim stems of silk roses even with angel's lace stems; if necessary, use florist's scissors to trim angel's lace stems even. Tie a bow around trunk of fan, concealing wire. Attach a craft-wire loop to back of fan for hanging.

Vine Wreath with Autumn Strawflowers

Materials:

* 12″ vine wreath and 8″ wire wreath
* 48 bunches wired strawflowers in assorted colors

Supplies:

* Wire: fine-gauge; craft
* Wire cutters

Note: This wreath is actually two wreaths in one: The floral wreath is set into the vine wreath.

Directions:

Wire flowers, one by one, to wire-wreath frame; cover frame completely. Set decorated wreath into center opening of vine wreath; wire together with fine-gauge wire. Form a loop for hanging from craft wire and attach to back of wreath.

Vine Wreath with Grape Clusters

Materials:

- 18″ grapevine wreath
- 3 artificial grape clusters
- 1 package each natural and teal eucalyptus stems
- 2½ yards Wedgwood-green wired ribbon

Supplies:

- Wire: fine-gauge; craft
- Florist's scissors
- Wire cutters
- Hot-glue gun and glue sticks

Directions:

Interspersing natural and painted stems, poke eucalyptus between vines at top center of wreath and hot-glue in place. Position grape clusters on wreath, two on left, one on right, and secure in place with fine-gauge wire. Tie bow, center, and hot-glue to top of wreath, allowing streamers to cascade in soft folds. Form a hanging loop from craft wire and attach to back of wreath.

French Horn with Evergreens

Materials:

- Brass or brasslike French horn with decorative cord and tassel
- Evergreen branches
- 2 pine cone and berry clusters
- 2½ yards red and green wide metallic ribbon

Supplies:

- Wire: fine-gauge; craft
- Wire cutters
- Pruning shears

Directions:

To form evergreen spray, bind evergreen branches at center with fine-gauge wire. Form a 6-loop bow with V-cut streamers; wire to center of spray. Wire 1 pine cone and berry cluster to each side of bow. Form a loop for hanging from craft wire and attach to back of evergreen spray.

Traditional Evergreen Wreath

Materials:

* 18″ pine wreath
* Fresh greenery
* 18 pine cones
* 12 red berries
* 2½ yards green brocade ribbon

Supplies:

* Wire: fine-gauge; craft
* Wire cutters
* Pruning shears

Directions:

Cut and position branches of fresh greenery on wreath; use fine-gauge wire to secure. Wire individual pine cones and berries, and attach to wreath foliage as desired. Arrange and attach ornaments. Finish with a bow wired to top front of wreath. Form a loop for hanging with craft wire and attach to back of wreath.

Further Reading

Condor, Susan. *Dried Flowers.* Boston: David R. Godine, 1988.

Hillier, Malcolm and Colin Hilton. *The Book of Dried Flowers.* New York: Simon & Schuster, 1986.

Ohrbach, Barbara Milo. *The Scented Room.* New York: Clarkson Potter, Inc., 1986.

Petelin, Carol. *The Creative Guide to Dried Flowers.* London: Webb & Bower, Inc., 1988.

Pulleyn, Rob. *The Wreath Book.* New York: Sterling Publishing Co., 1988.

__________ and Claudette Mantor. *Everlasting Floral Gifts.* New York: Sterling Publishing Co., 1990.

Sources

In addition to local florists, craft supply stores, and specialty shops that carry a selection of dried flowers and herbs, you may also want to contact:

Aphrodesia
282 Bleecker Street
New York, NY 10014

Caswell-Massey
58 Phipps
3500 Peachtree Road, N.E.
Atlanta, GA 30326

Caswell-Massey
Stonestown Galleria
3251 20th Avenue, Suite #107
San Francisco, CA 94132

Frank Holder
Box 78, Freedom Road
Pleasant Valley, NY 12569

Gilbertie's Herb Gardens
7 Sylvan Lane
Westport, CT 06880

Lewiscraft
40 Commander Boulevard
Scarborough, Ontario
M1S 3S2

Smith & Hawken
25 Corte Madera
Mill Valley, CA 94941

Tom Thumb Workshops
Route 13
P.O. Box 357
Mappsville, VA 23407

Index

Amaranth Bouquet, 52–54
Angel's Lace Fan with Silk Roses, 59–61

Cherub with Sweet Pea Wreath, 44
Cream and Persimmon Wreath with Print, 38–40

Decoration, 11–13
Design plans, 18–19
Dried flowers, 16–17

Empire Plume Wreath, 27–29

Faux Rose Topiary, 36
Foam, 11
Frames, 10, 16
French Horn with Evergreens, 66
Garden Rows, 47–49
Golden Branch Wreath, 24–26

Heart Wreath with Rose Clusters, 55–57
Hot-glue gun, 14

Materials, 10–14
Miniature Heart and Rings, 41–43
Moss, 16

Painted Vine Wreath with Rose Swag, 33–35

Straw, 11

Techniques, 14–17
Tools, 13–14
Traditional Evergreen Wreath, 69

Vine, 10
Vine wreaths, 14–15
Vine Wreath with Autumn Strawflowers, 62
Vine Wreath with Folk Dolls, 30
Vine Wreath with Grape Clusters, 64

White and Lavender Wreath, 21–23
Willow Wreath with Berry Swag, 51
Wire, 11
Wire-framed garland and wreath, creating of, 15

Metric Conversion Chart

1 inch	=	2.5 centimeters
1 foot	=	30 centimeters
1 yard	=	.9 meters